Watching Nature

Watching the Stars

By Edana Eckart

Welcome Books™

SCHOLASTIC INC.
New York Toronto London Auckland Sydney
Mexico City New Delhi Hong Kong Buenos Aires

ISBN 0-516-25232-1

12 11 10 9 8 7 6 5 4 3   5 6 7 8 9 10/0

Printed in the U.S.A.   61

First Scholastic printing, April 2005

Contents

There are many stars in the sky.

Our Sun is a star.

Many people use **telescopes** to look at stars that are far away.

Telescopes make stars look closer to us.

9

Scientists use very large telescopes to study stars.

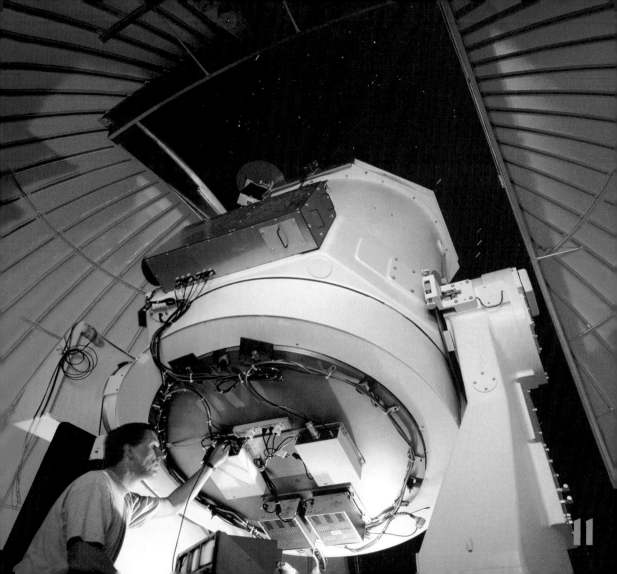

The large telescopes help scientists see stars that are very far away.

There is a telescope in **space** called the **Hubble Space Telescope**.

It takes pictures of stars.

For fun, we can make **shapes** with the stars in the sky.

Many stars together make up the shapes.

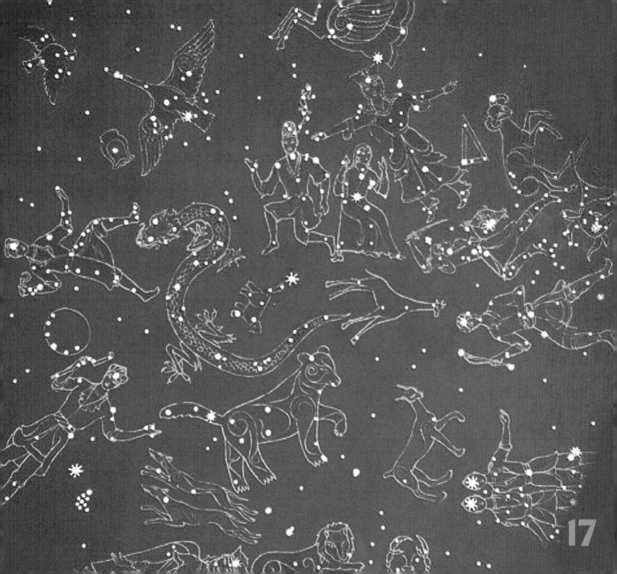

17

Some of the shapes have names.

One of them is called the **Big Dipper**.

It looks like a big **spoon**.

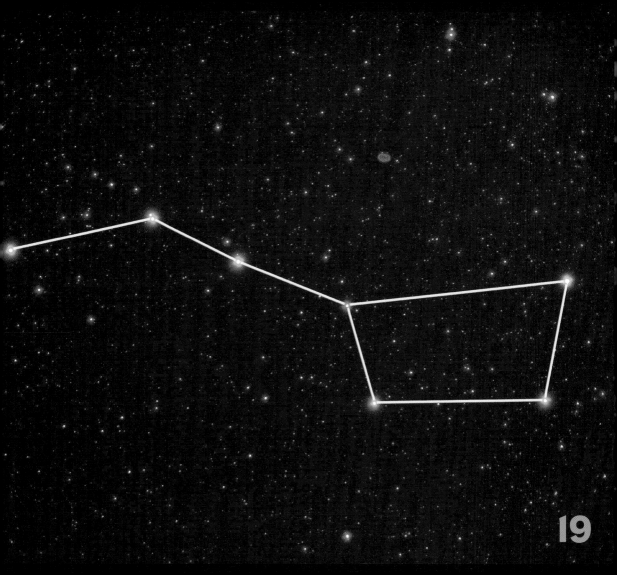

Many people enjoy watching the beautiful stars in the sky.

New Words

Big Dipper (**big dip**-ur) seven stars that are believed to make a picture in the shape of a spoon

Hubble Space Telescope (**huh**-buhl **spays tel**-uh-skohp) a telescope that circles Earth and takes pictures of stars and other things in outer space

scientists (**sie**-uhn-tists) people who have learned about some area of science and use it in their work

shapes (**shayps**) the way the outsides of things look, such as circles, triangles, and squares

space (**spays**) the area high above and all around Earth, where the Sun, planets, and stars are

spoon (**spoon**) a tool with a round part to hold food and a handle, used for eating some things

telescopes (**tel**-uh-skohps) instruments that make things that are very far away look larger and closer

To Find Out More

Book
Our Stars
by Anne F. Rockwell
Harcourt Children's Books

Web Site
Astronomy for Kids
http://www.dustbunny.com/afk/
Learn about the stars, play games, and more on this Web site.

Index

About the Author
Edana Eckart has written several children's books. She enjoys bike riding with her family.

Reading Consultants

Kris Flynn, Coordinator, Small School District Literacy, The San Diego County Office of Education

Shelly Forys, Certified Reading Recovery Specialist, W.J. Zahnow Elementary School, Waterloo, IL

Paulette Mansell, Certified Reading Recovery Specialist, and Early Literacy Consultant, TX